A

MW00652886

Other books by C. J. Sage

Poetry:

Let's Not Sleep (2002)

And We The Creatures

C. J. Sage
Editor

Dream Horse Press
California

Copyright © 2003 Dream Horse Press All Rights Reserved. No part of this publication may be reproduced or transmitted in any form or by any means, electronic or mechanical, including photocopy, recording, or any information storage or retrieval system, without permission in writing from the publisher. Permission requests and inquiries may be addressed to Dream Horse Press, Post Office Box 640746, San Jose, California 95164-0746.

Library of Congress Cataloging-in-Publication Data:

Sage, C. J.
    And We The Creatures / edited by C. J. Sage

          p.   cm
          Includes bibliographic references
          ISBN 0-9659307-5-0
          1. Poetry—Animal Rights
2002110798 2003
808.1—

10 9 8 7 6 5 4 3 2 1

First Edition

Printed in Canada

Frontispiece: The Bull by Franz Marc (Oil on canvas, 1911)
                courtesy of The Guggenheim Museum

Contents

To Hear the Falling World

Only if I move my arm a certain way,
it comes back.
Or the way the light bends in the trees
this time of year,
so a scrap of sorrow, like a bird, lights on the heart.
I carry this in my body, seed
in an unswept corner, husk-encowled and seeming safe.
But they guard me, these small pains,
from growing sure
of myself and perhaps forgetting.

— Jane Hirshfield

Foreword

So, if a man says to me, "Aren't those lambs pretty little creatures?" I answer 'No!' because his meaning, with his mouth full of lamb cutlets, is not my meaning.
—R. H. Blyth, "Joshu's Dog"

You have just dined, and however scrupulously the slaughterhouse is concealed in the graceful distance of miles, there is complicity.
—Ralph Waldo Emerson (Fate)

In general, I am not overly fond of theme anthologies. Like most readers, I want the most musically rapturous, conceptually engaging, and powerfully moving poetry I can find, and the putative subjects of those poems is a matter of slight importance. But that said, I must add at once that there are subjects so rare, and treatments of those subjects so useful that it makes perfect sense to put them between a single set of covers—especially if, as in this case, many of the poems are also finely made and musically deft. For me, poems that speak in significant terms of our relationship with other creatures, poems in which animals are not merely background or emblem or local color, but the explicit subjects of our meditations, fall into that category.

It has always seemed to me that compassion was in curiously short supply in 20th century American poetry: one can page through any number of thick collections of contemporary American verse without finding but a handful of poems in which the narrator moves outside his own ego to feel deeply for someone other than himself or a member of his own small tribe. It is to some extent precisely that rare virtue, the expression of a wider empathy, that makes political or social poetry of significant use. But even there, it is far more usual to sing of the anguish and suffering of one's own group.

Does not Walt Whitman remain our greatest poet, perhaps America's only sacred poet, not because he was a consummately skilled linguistic musician—which he certainly was—but because of precisely that generosity of spirit? "I do not ask the wounded person how he feels....I myself become the wounded person, / My hurt turns livid upon me as I lean on a cane and observe." Compassion, one of the Zen Patriarchs suggested, is the very manifestation of enlightenment.

And how much more interesting and useful when the poet manages to speak compassionately for creatures at once incalculably victimized and utterly voiceless, when our arguments with the world fully acknowledge our own constant victims, victims with whom we imagine we have so little in common and whom we often have the sentimental effrontery to imagine we love.

It is of some interest to note that pre-Christian philosophers of Greece and Rome agonized over the treatment of our fellow creatures in ways that most Judeo-Christian philosophers of the past two thousand years have been curiously incapable of doing. Empodocles (c.495-c.435 B.C.E.) preached vegetarianism on the basis of our kinship with animals; Theophrastus, Aristotle's pupil and successor, inveighed against both meat-eating and animal sacrifice as unnatural and unjust; Plutarch wrote two treatises in defense of animals, attempting in both to demonstrate animal intelligence; Ovid, Seneca and Plutarch also advocated the rights of animals while Porphyry's (C.E. 232-309) treatise "On Abstinence from Animal Food" attacked Christ for his indifference to animal suffering, pointing out that when Jesus transferred devils to the two thousand swine and cast them over a cliff, it was an act of gratuitous cruelty since his supernatural power could easily have found another way to cast out the devils.

In defense of the Judeo-Christian view of animals Augustine is the most intriguing apologist, not only accepting the argument that Christ had no regard for the pigs whom he cast over the cliff, but using the tale to prove that Christians have no obligation to treat animals with kindness. Acknowledging that "we see and appreciate from their cries that animals die with pain," Augustine argues, "man disregards this in a beast, with which, as having no rational soul, he is linked by no community of law." Although it is a view to which few of us would comfortably assent, it remains to a large extent, in practice, the sorry ethic by which we live. The nightmarish torture-chamber conditions of the typical factory farm, the horrors of the slaughterhouse, the anguish suffered by small creatures in animal testing labs, the gruesome and often trivial experiments that are the bread and butter of medical researchers are "justifiable" only because such creatures, despite all lip service to the contrary, ultimately do not count in the ethical code by which our own tribe lives. Surely nowhere is the distinction between the moral code we reserve for ourselves and the one we use for our neighbors more acute and venomous than here—in our bottomless cruelty toward our non-human brethren.

Of course there have always been poets who understood that larger fellowship. One thinks of those most visionary of our singers, people such as Burns, Smart, Whitman, Blake, and John

Clare, people who have taken the lives of other creatures seriously, poets who, in Whitman's words, "do not find the tortoise unworthy for not being something else." But to mention those few poets is to leave out the host of others, many of them our contemporaries, who have also attested to that larger fellowship.

The poets in this collection bear witness to precisely that kinship. Jane Mead, passing a truck full of chickens at night on highway 80, sees what most of us wish not to observe: "What struck me first was their panic./ Some were pulled by the wind from moving to the ends of the stacked cages,/ some had their heads blown through the bars—and could not get them in again. /Some hung there like that—dead—/ their own feathers blowing, clotting in their faces." Wesley McNair tells us quietly about the chained puppy down the road "who has not yet/ discovered he will spend his life there." Charles Harper Webb meditates on the impulse of young boys who "could not leave in peace/ creatures so graceful and self-contained." John Kennedy knows that now that the neighborhood is petitioning to get rid of the coyotes "no one's citing your loyalty/ to your mate anymore." Jane Hirshfield quietly blesses those "unstealthy bandits," the "little masked-face" raccoons, who gnaw in contentment on her garbage. Austin Alexis sees the white mice in the lab huddled together in their cage, "their complicated tails/ commingled as in love or/ an accelerated eagerness/ to aid each other/ before their clinical end." Stephen Dunn imagines a conspiracy in which animal spies have learned the terrible truth that humans "are savages" and that no one should "be fooled by their capacity for loving." Carl Rakosi, contemplating more somberly the daily horrors of the slaughterhouse, writes: "Gentle sheep/ I am powerless/ to mitigate your sorrow/ Men no longer weep/ by the rivers of Babylon/ but I will speak for you." Ashley Capps' sorrow has a more bitter edge; she offers no consoling trope when she addresses the neighbor cow in "I Used to See Her in the Field Beside My House," the one that is being readied for the rape rack and who will eventually be skinned and processed: "Old girl, there is nothing/ in this world that loves you back." And perhaps even more bitterly yet, Joe Duemer, seeing what his neighbor has done to his chained dog, seethes with unadulterated rage at humanity: "Let us kill one another/ with heedless abandon—we deserve it—/ but not the poor relations/ whose lives are without malice/ and whose motives are transparent." One is reminded of the terrifying line of poetry that got Robinson Jeffers into so much hot water with his readers: "I'd sooner, except the penalties, kill a man than a hawk."

C. J. Sage has assembled a collection of powerful and memorable poems, poems that bear witness to the terrors that other creatures suffer at our hands, and by doing so this thin volume raises the largest and most significant of questions. For all our self-aggrandizing pretense at universal compassion and a divinely-inspired ethics—a self-deception that would be merely ridiculous for its pomposity were it not so tragic—it is here, in such finely made poems, that we best learn the deepest secret of our own nature, that dark truth we most wish to deny. But by the same token, here too humanity's most ennobling feature, that longing to treat the world with tenderness and respect, manifests its power and grace.

In all, this is a fine anthology of poems touching on an essential, albeit little explored theme, and I wish the reader great pleasure—as well as some significant degree of shock, pity, anguish, and revelation—in reading it through.

— Steve Kowit

Some will say that no book of poetry limited to one topic, especially a political topic, can succeed as good literature. But others will say that all literature is political—that writers can never completely sterilize their work of personal politics. While there is certainly a balance to be struck, I think reasoning people will agree that their political sensibilities can tend to effect their literary senses. While I believe it *will* dazzle, this text should be read with more than just an expectation of bedazzlement within a literary neutrality. This book is an anthology of psalms—of praise realized and praise wished for the high regard of the non-human animal—and a treatise on the feasibility of fine 'political' poetry. Good literature does not ignore the world's realities, especially the sad realities. Yeats wrote that "All the words that I utter,/ And all the words that I write,/ Must spread out their wings untiring,/ And never rest in their flight,/ Till they come where your sad, sad heart is." The poet who addresses the heart behind personas may be among the most noble of poets.

Yusef Komunyakaa has defined poetry as "celebration and confrontation," and has said "everything is political."[1] Hayden Carruth says that "We are separated from the animals, which is part of our problem....I think that when the human race withdrew from the rest of the animals...we developed a sense of great sorrow and loss in our racial consciousness....I think that politics certainly belongs in poetry. It's in all the great poetry — *The Illiad* is a political poem, *The Divine Comedy* is a political poem, and *Paradise Lost*."[2] Horace believed that poetry should delight *and* instruct. Indeed, his call endures.

And We The Creatures is a collection of poems that may be deemed political, yes. But it is much more than that: it is an example of how politics and poetry *can* mix to make fine literature, and of how many of our finest contemporary poets are allowing a concern for animals to inform their work. This book will serve well as a classroom text or as a member of one's private poetry collection, as an animal rights study or simply a nature lover's companion. From this collection students will learn how to let their poetry sing not only their observations but also their thoughts and hearts, while poetry aficionados may discover exciting new facets of poets they've previously admired in other contexts. Within this collection animal lovers may find new levels of appreciation, and animal rights supporters will find they have extended family in the world of contemporary American poetry. The problem of animal abuse is not, unfortunately, limited to just a few societies. As many peoples across the globe know the mistreatment of animals, I hope this book will also inspire many more of its kind from many more places.

My sincere gratitude goes out to each publisher who gave permission for the reprints in *And We The Creatures*, and to Dream Horse Press for encouraging and publishing its first edition. Many thanks also, of course, to the excellent writers who generously contributed their work. It has been an honor and a pleasure to assemble this anthology and to work with such a wonderful, caring group of people. I hope the collection is as much a gift for its readers as it has been for me.

— C. J. Sage

Stephen Dunn

The Animals of America

The animals have come down from the hills
and through the forests and across the prairies.
They are American animals, and carry with them
a history of their slaughter. There's not one
who doesn't sleep with an eye open.

Out of necessity the small have banded
with the large, the large with the large
of different species. When dark comes
they form an enormous circle.

It's all, after years of night-whispers
and long-range cries, coming together.

To make a new world the American animals
know there must be sacrifices. Every evening
a prayer is said for the spies who've volunteered
to be petted in the houses of the enemy.
"They are savages," one reported,
"let no one be fooled by their capacity for loving."

ξ

The Puppy

From down the road, starting up
and stopping once more, the sound
of a puppy on a chain who has not yet
discovered he will spend his life there.
Foolish dog, to forget where he is
and wander until he feels the collar
close fast around his throat, then cry
all over again about the little space
in which he finds himself. Soon,
when there is no grass left in it
and he understands it is all he has,
he will snarl and bark whenever
he senses a threat to it.
Who would believe this small
sorrow could lead to such fury
no one would ever come near him?

ξ

Talking to the Dog

You can't say, I'm going away for a while
but I'll be back. When you say it
your wife calls from the next room,
"She's a dog — she doesn't understand."
Something's wrong is what she knows.
She wants to get in the car,
wants not to be left. Instead,
she refuses to look at you.
Is this sadness? Displeasure now,
sadness later? Or later only a room
with nobody in it, an odor, a noise,
the suspension of sleep.
She isn't thinking: Why has he left?
Was it my fault? She isn't a person.
She doesn't want to make you feel bad.

ξ

Abandoned Bluetick Bitch

Numbed with self-loathing,
we abandon the emissaries
of grace. Chained to a tree

beside the empty rental
she hollowed out a den
for herself & her young.

By the time we found her
the water they'd left her
was a couple of days gone.

When it was gone she would have
slept, not dreaming, letting the pups
nurse her sparse milk

& when the smallest died
she ate it to keep
her strength & cleanse the den,

depriving coy dogs & foxes
an expedient scent.
It's likely there were two more

before we found her.
Ribs covered by a tissue of dry skin,
she was nothing—a shadow

on the dirt & was just able
to raise her head & take
a little water from my hand

before turning to nose
her three live pups awake.
Reader, it is true, there is

horror everywhere worse
than this & cruelty that beggars
imagination, but this

is my horror, local & particular;
these were my neighbors did this,
who, without even the excuse

of racial or religious psychosis,
committed this wrong. Who live
in this same light & shadow I live in.

Let us kill one another
with heedless abandon—we deserve it—
but not these poor relations

whose lives are without malice
& whose motives are transparent.
Let us kill one another.

ξ

Chase Twichell

Aisle of Dogs

In the first cage
a hunk of raw flesh.
No, it was alive, but skinned.

Or its back was skinned.
The knobs of the spine

poked through the bluish meat.

It was a pit bull, held by the shelter
for evidence until the case
could come to trial,

then they'd put him down. The dog,
not the human whose cruelty

lived on in the brindled body,
unmoving except for the enemy eyes.

Not for adoption, said the sign.

All the other cages held adoptable pets,
the manic yappers, sad matted mongrels,
the dumb slobbering abandoned ones,

the sick, the shaved, the scratching,
the wounded and terrified, the lost,

one to a cage, their water dishes
overturned, their shit tracked around,

on both sides of a long echoey
concrete aisle—clank of chain mesh gates,
the attendant hosing down the gutters

with his headphones on, half-dancing
to the song in his head.

I'd come for kittens. There were none.
So I stood in front of the pit bull's
quivering carcass, its longdrawn death,

its untouched food, its incurable hatred
of my species, until the man with the hose
touched my arm and steered me away,

shaking his head in a way that said
Don't look. Leave him alone.
I don't know why, either.

ξ

Mourning for Rue

for Jim Stober

I know that you've been described as the spacy half-wit in the green house, but I saw your dead dog draped for three days over the mailbox for all the fast motorists to see. And the little sign below him that said, PLEASE SLOW DOWN. And suddenly I saw you Halloween, three years ago, dressed in a blue pinstriped suit wearing a real pumpkin over your head. You were grand, too. And you won first prize for costume. Later I heard that a couple people said they wouldn't have voted for you if they had known you were under there. I know that stinks and I know your sweet dog has left his body and that's just grief hanging there with a shiny collar around its neck. Christ, Jim, I'm helpless, too. George was run over on Chester Avenue in Bakersfield, 30 years ago, run over just like that, and Jimmy Duncan, who was never my friend, cried telling me. The way I see us right now we could both be dead, without our bodies, unable to reach down. Love, I think, lies somewhere between the wrist and the shoulder, Jim, a small red boat with immense stars overhead. There is the usual confusion, of course. Everyone is pointing. We are all on it.

ξ

Tormenting the Cat

For I will consider my Cat Geoffrey.
— Christopher Smart

Something about our cat's fastidious
licking made me want to mess him up.
Something about the perfect ring he made,

circling, kneading the couch with cushiony
gray paws to get the feel just right,
forced me to tug his tail and thump

his belly like a drum. His refusal
to come when I called made me clutch him —
squirming baby — to my chest.

His solemn face with phosphorescent eyes
and white whiskers made me knot
Susie's sun bonnet to his head,

and rubber-band a turkey feather to his tail.
His skittishness made me slam doors
to see him jump, or douse him

with the hose, then try to convince him
as he dashed up the sweetgum,
"It wasn't me." His desperate cries

for food encouraged me to hold his dish
above his head, inquiring,
"Want this, Kitty? Are you positive?"

Meaner boys than I kicked cats, sicked dogs
on them, lambasted trash dumpsters
with them inside. Sadists drenched strays

in kerosene, and watched them streak
like howling comets through the night.

None of us could leave in peace
creatures so graceful and self-contained,
so indulged and loved by women,
so indifferent as we writhed in our own flames.

ξ

The Fly

We watch John carefully tear off wings,
then all but one of the right legs.
We're young, but catch the knife's edge
curve of John's lips as he grins down at
our unlucky guest's attempts to walk away,
diminished to compass-circling, winding
us deeper and deeper into its hell.
Whether this is June or July now
doesn't matter — summer's over. No
one talks of how John's dad whipped that
treacherous fire into his eyes. No
one says, "No," and no one walks away.
Watching John in our tight arena,
we circle. We all laugh when he laughs.

Psalm

The sky is the red of the healing wound
of St. Agatha. New light
cast on the seven dead geese
stacked in the bed of the truck.
Their wings stiff around their bodies
make them cocoons of former flight.

The boy's breath, like a white wing,
hangs in the air above him.
His ears pink with wind,
the steel ridges of the truck bed
stripe his jeans with cold.
The sleeping dog rides in the back with him.
He can hear his father & two uncles
in the cab laughing. Their heads bob
between the guns on the rack.

On some of the geese the eyes are open.
A nonliving eye not quite clear,
like the clouded face of a watch.
He thinks of flying, how it would feel
to have nothing surround you.

You can hear their call
long before you see them.
He remembers hearing a flock
on another morning. Geese
stitched across the gray cloth of sky
just before the sun rose
red over the uneven mountains.

The birds flying over a boy's sleep,
distant voices lifting up memories—
the lull of silence after the rodeo, the bull
grazing with the clown's pony.

The grain sack full with struggling rabbits
slung over his shoulder, their vigorous feet
pounding his back as he walked
to the Saturday stock auction.
That distant call
made him want to be good.

The truck rattling over a cattleguard startles
the boy alert & he hears a moan.
At first he thinks it's the dog,
dreaming after birds.
But then another drone releases
from one of the geese.
He had watched them fall, spin around
& crumple like a kite in a dive,
dying in midair.

He sorts through the bodies,
black heads, pliant collared necks,
plush silvered breasts piled
limp & ruffled. He finds the goose
& holds it, unfolds the shut wings.
In the soft rush
of riffled feathers he feels
the clotted blood where the shot entered.

Opening the black visors of the bill,
he covers the nose holes with his fingers
& blows a few breaths of air
into the silty hollow of the bird.

And the dead bird gives back
the boy's own breath
in distinct syllables, nasal & conversational,
before the bill goes slack.

Then the boy breathes harder into the goose,
cradles it & listens
until there is music, a swell of air
returned over the bird's vocal chords, a purr,
a dirge, a lost-soul quaver.
A blue cone of sound, human-made,
or made human.

Advertisement for the Ford Explorer
for Mark Warburton

Both bumper and bison's horns point west
toward a blue range blurred in the distance,
which means that I'm to believe buying
an Explorer will validate my American character,
my ride humming with horsepower, a steel
coach to connote the grandeur of the bison.
But the bison is a stupid animal, the thin line
of drool hanging from its muzzle was airbrushed
out of the picture and is now just a patch of grass,
grass it would eat if permitted by the photographer
and team of bison-handlers just out of view.
The Explorer looks glossy and new, of course,
for it was just helicoptered from a dealership
to the butte-top and buffed by professionals
who specialize in automotive makeovers.
The bison looks worn by comparison, its dun
muzzle of curls, its horns blunt with use,
which makes me think that we are animals
more stupid than the bison, we who shot them
from horses and trains for target practice:
men who howled and poured gin, who aimed
their rifles and swapped bills as bison
fell with muffled grunts along the prairies.
It is strange how "progress" exterminated the bison
from this land, transformed it into a victim
of its own dumb nature, an ideal American emblem.
I would like to choose the bison over the Ford Explorer
(which is my birthright as an American shopper),
and I would pet the poor beast, whisper to him,
lead him away from his handlers and photographers.
I would walk him home to my garage and hose
down his back, wax his horns, shoo away boys
who glide by on their bikes and take aim at him
with guns made from their thumbs and index fingers,
squinting eyes, hammers snapped with a pow.

David Roderick

"Dominating the Field," states the ad for the Ford Explorer,
but I doubt that the bison ever thought to dominate
anything other than the patch of grass beneath it.
My bison just wants to stand in my suburban yard,
out of focus, odd among the tiny starlet clovers,
grunting and drooling and glad for his simple life.

ξ

The Bear on Main Street

What made the man kill this bear?
His truck, across which the bear's body lies,
tells me it wasn't to feed his family
or because his children were cold.

The bear has beautiful black feet, delicate
almost, like the soles of patent leather slippers,
and the wind riffles the surface of its fur
with the sheen of water in the autumn sun.

The bear looks as if it might only be sleeping,
but its tongue lags from its mouth, and the man
has wrapped it with stout twine and bound it
to the bed of his truck,
as if he were afraid it might speak.

Three teenage boys pull their pickup to the curb.
One of the boys guesses what the bear must weigh.
Another wants to know how many shots it took,
and the third boy climbs down. He strokes its nose
   and forehead.
He traces the bear's no longer living skull
with the living bones of his fingers
and wonders by what impossible road
he will come to his father's country.

ξ

David Baker

The Deer

How long did we watch? How long did those
three deer stand pondering the dark, bowing to taste
the least brown grasses, the cold-burnt rosehips,
and whatever else kept alive by the creek?
I think of them each time we lie down, just so.
How still they could stand and still tremble.
They had walked out of the woods one by one.
They leaned to dry earth as to drink.
I think of them when we lie long minutes
through the reaches of winter, not lost ourselves,
not thirsty. How our bodies tense to be touched
when we forage in a scatter of blankets.

Once a man laid a deer flat with a single shot.
This gets easier to say. You open both eyes.
You let out your breath and stay still, no matter
how cold the wind, no matter how dark or how near.
The man, who is dead now, couldn't help but smile.
He walked to where the deer fell and kept as to drink.
I think of them when we lie down like this.
We watched three deer lost under cedars so long
we saw the wind hold still and the ruffle of fur
behind each tense shoulder over each heart was like
our bullet digging in. That's how long. That's how still.
Until our will to love was also our power to kill.

ξ

I Used to See Her in the Field Beside My House

Perhaps it is the way your nipples,
long like fingers on an open hand,
beckon the tired, huddled, osteoporosis-fearing
masses to your swollen, steaming milk sack.

The skin of your huge behind ripples
where giant horseflies understand
only that you taste good, not that they hurt you while you're looking
at the vast and swirling pasture through a crack

in your stall. Cow, listen— forget the deep pools
of rain that pock the lit, green landscape of your youth. Forget the singing
man who rubbed your head. He's readying the rape rack.

In the end, you're skinned and processed. A hip pulls
loose, shoulders dismantle in the hands
of some masked worker. Old girl, there is nothing
in this world that loves you back.

ξ

"Cows on modern dairy farms are repeatedly artificially inseminated on what farmers call "the rape rack." The milk they produce to feed their young is taken several times each day by machines that irritate their sensitive udders, leading to mastitis and infection. Their male calves are taken from them and chained in tiny veal crates, where they spend 16 weeks barely able to move, before being slaughtered."

—Animal Times Magazine, PETA

John Kennedy

Gently Close

The nearness of them was enough
to keep us from church, though another
family might honk *move along*
as we inched up to the troughs thinking
then shouting GUERNSEYS
from the car windows, the practiced
first syllable a barrel of cow mimicry

rising from the wells of our throats
until we ran out of air and the 2nd
quieter syllable resolved
into a pair of Zs winging
for the high open fields where deer
sometimes slipped out
of the landscape looking

as if they were caught moments
after a kiss. The cows, however,
never showed a hint of
enchantment, were down-
right agnostic about transformations.
Oh they knew better—if that's
what domesticated sense is—

than trying to leap the fences
and stone walls that time
or circumstance builds, them huddling
gently close, not tempting
what had them tramping mud and bearing
the indignity of odor
as they leaned on each other

like the best of friends.
The eyes a cut of sunless water,
disparately thin legs fighting

for equilibrium, the way people standing
on a bus have to, and the udders
swaying like traveling bags, tugging
them earthward, to all things sensible.

ξ

Cows

The cows are lowing and the moon is a crescent.
It is the 21st day of July.
The year doesn't matter. The weather
doesn't matter. The nighttime hardly matters.
I could listen to the cows
with my own mouth pressed to the block, how animals
know what is happening to them
even when it hasn't. How the back of someone's neck
can be a window to the soul—forget the eyes
which are practiced. I could keep listening
to the lowing my friend detests.
He has a skeptical sense of the sacred
and the cows are ugly
he says. I think they are beautiful
like Beethoven
or a Chevrolet. I want to kiss them
under the crescent moon
in my neighbor's pasture
and tell my friend how sorrowful
it all was, there in the weatherless
night where I do not know
what matters and I do not know what will happen.

ξ

Christmas Lambs

By the road in the meadow,
a dozen lambs, still damp from birth,
umbilical cords dangling
like fluorescent pink roots from soft undersides,
stagger on black legs through the frosty grass.

It's the first day of winter
on the North Coast,
a wet world of lush green, and unexpected white.
This morning snow fell (in a place where snow never falls)
into the ocean,
and over the trees, covering the redwoods in lace.

The lambs, uncomplaining, shiver and suckle.
They know nothing other than this,
and believe in
the glistening green meadow dotted with lumps of white,
the sly and frosty radiance of blue sky above,
golden light slanting down sharply through snowy sugar pines,
their mothers force-bred out of season.

A ewe, trailing her placenta like a bloody flag,
rump swollen from the birth,
glares with a stupid woolly sheep face,
ridiculous and pathetic in her pain.
In the spring she will cry incongruously
for her twin lambs sent to slaughter.
Then she will be bred again.

How easy it is to be fooled into
miracles. New life, innocent lambs,
golden sun. The excitations of nature,
an ocean inexplicably full of snow.
Joyous, we can't imagine that exact moment
weeks from now when the snow vanishes like a dream,

and the Christmas lambs are hacked to pieces
any more than know how crazy
luck can quickly pierce our own lives
on a glorious Christmas morning,
trouble sharp and shining just beyond the treetops.

ξ

No One Talks About This

They go in different ways.
One hog is stationed at the far end
of the pen to decoy the others,
the hammer knocks the cow
                    to his knees,
the sheep goes gentle
            and unsuspecting.
Then the chain is locked
around the hind leg
and the floor descends
                    from under them.
Head down they hang.
The great drum turns
the helpless objects
and conveys them slowly
to the butcher waiting
at his station.
The sheep is stabbed
behind the ear.

Gentle sheep, I am powerless
to mitigate your sorrow.
Men no longer weep
                    by the rivers of Babylon
but I will speak for you.
If I forget you, may my eyes
lose their Jerusalem.

ξ

Jane Mead

Passing a Truck Full of Chickens
at Night on Highway Eighty

What struck me first was their panic.

Some were pulled by the wind from moving
to the ends of the stacked cages,
some had their heads blown through the bars—

and could not get them in again.
Some hung there like that—dead—
their own feathers blowing, clotting

in their faces. Then
I saw the one that made me slow some—
I lingered there beside her for five miles.

She had pushed her head through the space
between bars—to get a better view.
She had the look of a dog in the back

of a pickup, that eager look of a dog
who knows she's being taken along.
She craned her neck.

She looked around, watched me, then
strained to see over the car—strained
to see what happened beyond.

That is the chicken I want to be.

ξ

In Your Honor

In your honor, a man presents a sea bass
tied to a black-lacquered dish by green-spun seaweed.

"Ah" is heard throughout the room:
you are unsure what is about to happen.

You might look through a telescope at the full
bright moon against deep black space,

see from the Bay of Dew to the Sea of Nectar,
but, no, this beauty of naming is a subterfuge.

What are the thoughts of hunters driving
home on a Sunday afternoon empty-handed?

Their conception of honor may coincide
with your conception of cruelty? The slant

of light as sun declines is a knife
separating will and act into infinitely thin

and lucid slices. You look at the sea bass's eye,
clear and luminous. The gills appear to move

ever so slightly. The sea bass smells
of dream, but this is no dream. "Ah,

such delicacy" is heard throughout the room,
and the sea bass suddenly flaps. It

bleeds and flaps, bleeds and flaps as
the host slices slice after slice of glistening sashimi.

ξ

Sushi

Pared to a near essence, a mere
intention, his motions
flow with the off-handed grace
of mating jellyfish, arms oddly beefy,
smooth as anything loved too much
by the sea. Fingers chilled
to a pale rice color, he eases
a moon-streak of knife through thick flesh
clean as the shark's fin splitting the air,
untouched by hesitation, shaving
rich steaks with more consistency
than a calm lake slaps its shore.
Each spoonful of uni, heaped
upon a finger-width of rice,
luminous moons atop a backdrop
of black lacquer, begs the question
what nourishes more, fish
or artifice, consumption
or consummation of a flesh both
raw and fully perfected, spiced
by the mastery of his hands made
vassal to our hunger? Reminiscent
of nothing that teems and multiplies,
the tongues of ahi nonetheless speak
to something in our sea-swollen vessels
still tugged at by the sea and something
in our souls with no taste
for the bodily, oddly embarrassed
by the need, the act, of eating.
Inscrutable in squid-white apron, he
leads us, lures us, to the source,
presents something so nearly still
swimming, we can all but taste
its last sensations, its final desire:

not to die, not for us, not to finish
its life of feast and fleeing sliced
upon the cutting board of time to serve
something like a god, but more
sensual, more ravenous, more
likely to want more than we are.

ξ

The New Fish Store

Can the neighborhood sustain
the pride of the new fish store?
In the window
on a bed of crushed ice they make
still lives of dead fish.
The walls are new linoleum tile,
the plastic flowers are fresh.
Under a picture of Jaws the shark it says
Get even, eat a fish.
There are calendars of Greece,
there are fly-casting paintings
with trout flying in loops
there are plastic lobsters
there are nets and corks, all clean.
One person waits on you
another cleans the fish
a third takes your money
so the hand that touches money
will never touch your fish.
On New Year's Eve, on the ice is spelled
HAPPY NEW YEAR in silver smelts.

ξ

Harbor Seals

Kill them
if you want to, say, if you're
a fisherman and you think
seals are too good
at catching the fish *you* want,
fish that put food on your family's table.
That's pretty good reasoning. All you need
is a small rifle
and one good eye. Just be sure
you do it quick. It's embarrassing enough
to come across a dead one on the beach,
it's worse to come across one dying.
The one I found had little more
than a scratch across the back of its neck
that sent a dark line of blood
into the sand. A seal's eyes are liquid anyway,
and alert right to the end. When the sea mist
is fine and constant, a seal
can stay beached for hours without
drying out. You don't have to believe
any of this. I sat down close to the idiot
thing, and waited with it for the tide.

The Bisbee Donkeys

Lowered in by pulleys and belts, donkeys were once used in the Bisbee Mine to haul carts of ore. Some lived as long as seventeen years in the mine. Most went blind.

Going down, they must've kicked,
fighting for a last breath of real air, a final
glimpse of light. Below,
they must've stumbled over iron-rutted tracks
until darkness thickened, shadows disappeared.

Here I should just tell myself
animals don't reason, can't differentiate
between justice and fate,
have no knowledge of dust,
how it packs lungs, smothers desire.

I should say they have no memories
of wet, green grass. Still,
beneath bright planets, a dispassionate moon,
if only for an afternoon, an occasional night,
the miners could've hauled the donkeys out.

And here, I could change the story,
write that they did. But I prefer to think
of those men as incapable
of such cruelty. They wouldn't haul
the donkeys out, only to drag them back,

considering, especially, the newest arrivals
who knew only a mother's shaggy flanks,
her black milk, born
into the palpable pitch
out of whatever instincts that, even if hobbled,

nevertheless break free.
How blinding all that sudden light would be,
the unfathomable blue.

A kindness then. By the men
who day after day had to coldly
ratchet themselves down, descend,
Stygian, with shovel and axe,
the pinpricks of their lanterned miners' hats
a constellated sky brought underground:
distant celestial animals, fixed, wheeling.

ξ

Memorials of Names as Plain as Land

Such scant small souls, dry leaves like birds take flight.
From edges of the road they sail the sun
to rise and reel then float and land, each one
as light as breath of clouds, as fleet of sight.
A carriage stands as if the farmer left it
for a moment while he went for some forgotten thing.
These trees have ringed a hundred years
the barnyard where the horses rest;
perhaps the kin of those who pulled the plow
and hauled the logs to build this place,
their graves unmarked. They worked from dawn
to dusk, these slaves of field and farm,
their willingness forgotten now except
that some have passed their bloodlines down:
a blaze of white along the head and hoof
or a certain way they hold themselves aloof
like ghosts of Molly, Mr. Pease and Browne.

ξ

The Horse's Life

The cowboy-poet has written many lines
      praising the virtues of his horse.

He believes his animal has a loyal heart
      and a soul—that one day it will rise

from tired flesh to a heaven of high grass
      and wait for him, saddled, ready to serve.

ξ

Ellen Bass

Bears In China

*More than 7000 bears are currently imprisoned for their bile
which is used to produce shampoos, aphrodisiacs and "miracle" remedies.*

Anyone can find it on the internet—the bear
crushed into the wooden cage, flattened
like a rug, folded and packed for transport.
The eyes, staring out the small openings, are alive,
are suffering. And the snout pushes out
through one lashed corner. If it weren't
a real bear, if it weren't pinned flat,
the crate so tight it cannot scratch,
twenty years lying in its urine and feces,
if it didn't have a small hole pierced
in its belly, with the dark hair shaved
so it looks like a pale iris,
like a terrified eye, the pupil
shrunk almost to nothing, if a tube
were not stuck through that cut
and if bile were not sucked out
like the insides of an egg, and if
the bear did not roar, not even
in the beginning, and did not bite
himself, and did not eat the food
by his five-toed paw or stretch his tongue
to the drops of water on the bar,
and if the massive body had not turned
a deaf ear on the longing of the soul
to die, if what was in that box
was only the fur of a bear, scraped
of its fat, its flesh hot stew
in the stomachs of children, the hide
worked supple, the heavy claws intact,
then could we climb into that skin
and become the bear? Could we know
what it knows? If we walked
through our lives, draped
in the tremendous coat of the bear, all
our actions would carry its sorrow.

ξ

Elephant Waltz

Abishag, Dido, Clemence, and Nadezhda,
a circle, a square,
then two elephant pairs with a kissing of trunks,
and the music of two foolish tubas
galumphs through the ring,
a waltz with the pulse of an elephant's heart
to disguise their great silence.
Step left step right and sway, shift the great weight
upon the tough pads of their feet
and their high loose knees,
and the audience thinks they are waltzing.

But this is the dance of two hundred war elephants—
step left and turn—
as they wait for the armies of great Alexander
to ford the Hydaspes
with war cries half drowned by the rain,
wait for the pain and the panic,
their mahouts slip dead from their backs
and the javelins sting—circle right,
in a stench not of popcorn but blood
and the terrified horses, slide left
in the mud of the monsoon.
The river is rising.

And this is the dance
of a Bombay–Burma Trade Limited elephant—
softly step forward—
hauling a thirty-foot four-ton teak log
in between stubs of the forest and through the bamboo,
her wooden bell muttering under her chin,
along a wet precipice—back and step forward.
And if the log rolls she must whirl back and lower her head
so the harness will peel itself over her face
like the shrug of a girl's nylon slip,

and the teak will go over without her.
One more slow circle.
Abishag, Dido, Clemence, and Nadezhda
go to their knees, they lower their heads.
The audience thinks they are bowing.

ξ

The Acts of the Elephants

Sound of a mountain murmuring in its sleep
drew Timothy to his window in the pale part of the night
where he saw the humps of dawn-colored elephants pass,
saw the loose strides that took them down the street
quietly, almost in step, and the dream
he stood in went with them to the edge of town.
They bore it with everything else that makes them so heavy.

They were not exactly running away,
since every day they went back to the wagons,
but every night for two weeks they escaped
through town to green New Jersey, a wide place with trees.
Every night in the place where the ground was moist
Dido planted her foot in last night's footprint,
then Abishag did, Nadezhda, and Clemence.

They have to be large, with all they don't forget.
The claws that fit these scars, the iron cuff too small for this leg,
centuries of work and war, winters of crusted ice,
sweetness of yellow grass when the crust gave way.
The waltz and gallop. They render it all
in pendulous vats of stomach and long, long guts.
In a week the widened footprint filled with water.

They stuffed their mouths with fiddlehead ferns
and wet striped maple leaves. They scratched every itch.
Eased out loaves of dung, flicked mud on their shoulders.
Tim may have seen them dance on Sunday in pink and green satin;
by now he's not sure. That year the lake was born.
His stepsons take him there to sail little boats
that start out bravely and don't know how to come back.

ξ

Sommer's Fur Farm

Were I to follow this homemade
logo on its truckbed of plywood
empty almost as the crates it carries
ignoring even my turn-off for work
surely would be revealed a lane
mud ruts with sunflowers
on one side and corn on the other
winding like a dry creekbed
to conifers surrounding outbuildings
and a barn in the dead of Wisconsin

I might speak now of a black caterpillar
crawling on the skull of a bald man
cows that cough up hair balls
a lawn long gone to seed
a mink pitch fork
the bearskin rug
in the farmer's den and
the fur-lined cups and saucers
in the kitchen we sip
pretend cups of coffee from
picking in midst of conversation
first fuzz and now dust from the bread

ξ

Byzantine Bird
for Q

Back in the ruins of Byzantium,
I went to market & explored a stand
that sold canaries, where I stood & watched

a golden songbird with a chartreuse breast
pound his little marmalade-crested head
against the bars of his far-from-gilded cage.

My chest tightened in the open air,
& I got claustrophobic when I saw
how he would beat his black-lined wings as if
the sky were not beyond his reach for good.

Frantic & panic-stricken though he looked,
he launched into a song out of the blue,
his consolation for his pain a joy
to hear. I left him behind bars of music.

ξ

Austin Alexis

Witness

The wise gray men
conspire in the lab.
The sanitized whiteness
of their lab coats
does not blind me
to the stain of their deed:
enticement of white mice
unto death, to verify a theory.

See the Corinthian jumble,
the sculptural lump
of their complicated tails
commingled as in love or
an accelerated eagerness
to aid each other
before their clinical end.

ξ

Narcosis Song

There was another sea, outside,
wrapped around me;

savage waves and old kelp
were rocking arms.

Hunger and fear were fibers
of its endless soft net —

captured by the hands
of a stranger who pierced it,

I swallowed a piece
as a last sweet secret.

At night I sigh
that stolen mesh unfurled

to cloak me in my dreams,
and each morning when I wake

within the sudden dawns of glass,
I swallow again.

I have fallen through a hole
in an old weave, to the surface

of a small, thirsty earth —
into a nightmare, or unfinished hunt.

ξ

Most ornamental saltwater fish are taken from the wild, often from depths requiring that a needle be inserted into their bladders to release the gas caused by being brought to the surface. 'Needled' or not, most do not survive even their shipment to wholesalers or pet stores. Those who do survive the trip usually suffer captivity-related illnesses followed by slow death in home or office aquariums.

Pet Shop

People are wandering the aisles
looking for a pet. I am there
in the back with the silence

attending the fish and stones
who know about the false
currency under our tongues.

Even the walking-sticks disappear
among the reeds. They know we are thieves,
having stolen the fruit, water, fire . . .

Our grandmothers are live
ash, long white braids of smoke
rising into the hole in the sky,

leaving unrecognized by our children,
who continue trying to catch
anything that moves.

No loitering. Do not touch.
You break, you pay.
When no one is looking

I offer my fingertips.
Gold surfaces from the dark.
Lips, soft as an infant's ears.
All day and all night
people tapping the glass,
desire to see, to be seen.

ξ

Sarah Lindsay

Slow Butterflies in the Luminous Field

In this kennel you'll see our most popular cross:
golden retriever with Red Delicious apple.
The apple genes make 'em glossy and calm
and symmetrical. They travel well,
don't jump, don't run around, don't bark.
Frankly, we didn't expect their teeth
to be so soft, but they do just fine on mush.
Handsome, aren't they?

                            Down that hall
are miniature poodles with parrot genes,
bright blue with yellow eyes. The night shift
taught this batch to say Help! I'm being held prisoner
in a fortune cookie factory!
It was funny the first hundred times.

This room will be for hamster turtles.
The pet stuff may not change the world,
but we can't do that without income, right?

Now in this paddock we're saving the rhino
by making it woolly again. With vicuña genes,
it's relatively docile, it's fluffy, lots of square footage—
mark my words, rhino fleece will be hot.
And look at those Bambi eyes—who goes on safari
to shoot a cream puff like this?

Most of our projects are in development.
In here we're working with kudzu genes in silkworms
to increase the output and tensile strength,
but so far we've only doubled their appetite.
And the spider-barnacle thing has yielded
intriguing results, but nothing we're ready to publish.

But out here—you should see this field in the evening

when we let the butterflies out.
Looks like ordinary tobacco, doesn't it,
but those leaves are making insulin as we speak.
We also incorporated a jellyfish gene.
That's for the butterflies, which are part slow loris—
that way they can't start hurricanes by fluttering,
or migrate to where their forests used to be.
When the butterflies turned out nocturnal too,
we figured we'd make the tobacco plants glow in the dark.

At night they give off a pale green light,
and bow their heads, from a bluebell cross, I think,
to be pollinated more easily,
and the butterflies walk in slow motion up the stalks.
Their wings open and close every minute or so;
maybe they think they're flying. And the plants
move their leaves a little, too,
as if they were shifting in a summer breeze,
as if there were any more breezes.

ξ

Cheese Penguin

The world is large and full of ice;
it is hard to amaze. Its attention
may take the form of sea leopards.
That much any penguin knows
that staggers onto Cape Royds in the spring.
They bark, they bow one to another,
she swans forward, he walks on her back,
they get on with it. Later
he assumes his post, an egg between his ankles.

Explorers want to see everything, even
the faces of penguins whose eggs have been stolen
for science. At night they close the tent flaps
to fabricate sundown, hunch together
over penguin fried in butter, and write up their notes.
Mornings they clump over shit-stained rocks,
tuck eggs in their mittens, and shout.
Got one, got one. They shove back their balaclavas;
they feel warm all over.

The penguins scurry for something to mother,
anyone's egg will do, any egg
no matter how stiff and useless the contents,
even an egg-shaped stone to warm—
and one observer slips to a widow
a red tin that once held cheese.
Finally the wooden ship sails, full of salted penguin,
dozens of notebooks, embryos,
explorers who missed as little as possible. But:

The penguin cherished the red tin on her feet.
She knew what was meant to happen next
and she wanted it, with a pure desire
refined for thirty-five million years
in the dark eye of every progenitive cell.

And it happened. A red tin beak broke through
and a baby flopped into the rock nest, smelling of cheese—
but soon he was covered with guano, so that was all right.
Begging for krill from his aunts' throats just like the others.

Winter: blue ice, green ice, black sea,
hot breath of yellow-jawed killer whales.
Summer: pink slime on black rock,
skuas that aim for the eye. Krill, krill,
a shivering molt, krill, krill, a mate,
and so on. And though he craved dairy products
he never found any; though he was miraculous
no one came to say so. The world is large,
and without a fuss has absorbed stranger things than this.

ξ

Who'll Say Dugong When the Dugong's Gone?

Kiss a mermaid while you can.
They're twelve feet long
and have bones thick as ivory.

The myth-conception began
when sailors, rummed or simply
craving beauty, confused

the sixteen-hundred-pound dugong
for a glistening woman in fins.
Because the dugong's almost

extinct, mermaids will soon
abandon our stories. Already
we don't quote the Cyclops

or ask the Minotaur to drinks.
Remember this rule
from economics: less is less

interesting. Subtract
the dugong with its one hair
per square inch from Kupang

Bay and Arakan Reef, take
the snow leopard and the snow
itself and soon we'll have Cleveland

from here to the Antilles.
The dugong swims and eats and makes
dugongs, it's a shadow

within the shadow of the sea
and not us, reason enough
for it to live. Sometimes

Bob Hicok

I think the bulldozer's how we say
that only the world we make
is real. There are nights

I try to grow a beard & hook,
try to let stars burn a map
on the inside of my skull

as I rise and fall on the breath
of water, I'm the kind
of sailor who'll walk the plank.

On my way down I want to see
that whiskered face, not human
but calm, a mammal happy

to be where it happens to be,
which is joy and something
you'd never say about us.

ξ

"Spawned-Out Chinooks Aid Future Generations from the Afterlife"
—National Fisherman news service, January 19, 1999

It could be harder. We could be in the water, seam-ripping the river, homing in
on the growing molecules of scent, that taste of home's fir needles steeped
in the steep stream. We would be starving, dying, battered back by constant cascades.

But if we were in the water, both of us would be light and alive, writhing and fluttering
together, a team. No, I would be unnecessary, and you'd be where you should be,
not in an olive drab rucksack. You're heavy, dead. The dry ice is a mixed blessing.

This spring we're hauling eight tons of you back to Chinook Pass, to the Bumping River,
the American, the Naches, dumping you back to rot. From the Hanford Reach
to the Upper Yakima, a thousand of you, trucked-in, hiked-in ghosts.

Your absence here lately has caused many hungers. No spawned-out salmon,
no rotting flesh, no maggots, no insects, no protein to feed the fingerlings
come spring. So we piggyback you home, past the dams, past the farms,

past the pavement, up the Forest Service roads, past clearcuts that suffocate
the long allee to your birth place and death place. We lay you in the stream, hope briefly
for the wiggling, adamant flap of departure, but watch the wide, still eye float away.

The river will loll you down. When the weather turns warmer you will rot.
And the young will rise to the wealth of your death. And maybe
they will come back on their own. And maybe they won't.

ξ

Sarah Lindsay

His Hot Breath on Her Cheek

Delicately they select the wet mangrove tangle,
island where nothing is dry, and the barrier reef
they will study to save. One will dangle
on bubble umbilicus down the shocking blue cliff,

tearing gorgonian fans from the fractal wall:
See how it changes color, see how it closes.
Another bands plastic bags of dye over coral;
X-rays later ask how it took its doses.

Another with coral blocks set between his knees
slowly hammers out their secret worms,
another irradiates blue-green and calcareous algaes
and tinily slices the great Greek brown sponge urns,

two more plot the extensive line of holes
for informative cores sucked out by submarine drills,
one anoints clams with relaxing chemicals
so they open, open to his eyes as if they willed.

The transparent amphipod with salt-spoon claws
drifts glistening across the tabled slide.
Gravely the microscope attends its nerves,
its delicate sac of red beneath black eyes.

Now, bent upon the tank where they re-create
all reef conditions, calculable and mutable,
a tender love-light ripples in their faces.
I understand you now. You beautiful.

ξ

Panda Passing

She's going, her panda
spirit finally returning
to China. No trap
of laws can hold her—

the body is what she
leaps out of. The zoo
looks strange. Now
she can roam where
her ancestors roamed
before missionaries
and guns came. People

cry over empty spaces
where cameras have
nothing to aim for. She
can't hear them.

A river swings
into view. Grass. Small
indigo flowers around
her paws. As wind
meets her fur, she
climbs a rusty hill

where the sun is gold
straw in an owl's nest.

ξ

Adam & Eve Go to the Zoo

It is Adam who stops at the front gate
Even though it's open and held back.
He quivers, like he's thought of a splinter.
Eve is already looking past the iron gates
Into the plotted wilderness that aches
Inside of her like a vague déjà vu.

There is the walrus, there is the fox,
There is the panda and his hiding box.

Adam is drawn to bears: the bloated mass
Of brown fur, heavy-pawed. He feels this way:
Without dexterity. Yet Adam is
In awe of the secret nimbleness their fingers
And his contain. He wonders if someone, maybe
Even Eve, will ask to see how they work.

Eve finds herself pressed against the glass
Of the gorilla, bigger than she,
Who she imagines she could fit inside,
The swell of child, or the ultraviolet
Blossom of soul. She hopes that maybe the bee
Will see what is beyond her vision now.

Here is the goat, here is the lamb,
Here is the camel with his head in the sand.

Here is Adam in the butterfly
Enclosure, disappointed by the silence.
Eve comes upon him here, and the monarchs come
And nest in her hair. She feels as if the wind
Has visited her; and Adam takes one on
His finger and lets Eve give it lift with breath.

The nursery, at last: egg-white and full
Of murmur; the cub is suckling milk
From a bottle; bright new sheep for the grasslands
Tumble; Adam and Eve are still at last
(Their breath marks on the glass). This is
The world that they were born for, if not born into.

Here is the woman, here is the man.
Here is the earth in the palm of our hand.

ξ

Jason Gray

The Snow Leopard
In the MetroToronto Zoo
-for Paul Strong

He pads on grassy banks behind a fence,
   with measured paces slow and tense.

   Beyond his cage his thoughts are sharp and white;
   he lives a compelled anchorite.

   A solid ghost gone blind with all the green,
   he waits and waits to be unseen.

ξ

Zoo Vigil

We dream jungle, we dream veld. Where
elephants now go to die: bare ground
fenced between calligraphied giraffes
and the tender-eyed okapi. An elephant

lies in state: a kind of earthen wake for
the living, who lumber in needful ritual,
knowledge in their silent feet,
their arcane, undomesticated bones.
They grieve in a dusty oval,
touch their comrade again and again

to make sure that he is dead, to lay
their peace upon him, gather his peace
unto themselves. Hour upon hour
they circle him and touch him,
the friable ground wreathing up

all that can shade eternity back to them,
whatever more than dust
may spread safekeeping.

ξ

57

When Peacocks Scream

They suddenly appeared,
the two of them,
in suburbia, Chicago, in the hot of the summer.

Two peacocks
in the middle of a soccer field
housed in a cage that looks out only to the east.

The *pras*, Buddhist monks, fed them
carrots and lettuce,
grown in the garden outside their cage.

They screamed
when the trucks rumbled out of the truck yard,
blaring on their horns.

They screamed
when the Thai children pleaded with them
to fan open, banging on the cage with insistent fists.

They screamed
at night, the *pras* running, half their robes on,
out of the temple, hoping their racist neighbors hadn't killed them.

When they fanned open,
only when the day was most quiet, they danced around each other,
a tango of the blue from the China Sea and green of a jade Buddha.

The two of them,
forever mates, huddled close on a mound of hay,
necks entwining, always waiting for the sun to rise,

but never able to see it set.

ร

How I Learned That My Feet Must Always Be On The Ground

Magpie the trickster makes a mistake,
flies in, I don't know why,
then says, "Gotta get out!
Gotta get out!" bashing the windows
where Sky seems to be waiting.
I chase Magpie round and round the room,
ceiling to floor, window to window,
and when I finally catch him,
he has blood on his head
and trembles in my hands.
I think of him as prize, as prisoner,
and make a step to take him to my friend,
when suddenly he stirs, whirs away,
and everything happens all over again.

The mistake was mine, not his.
I leap for him and grab
only a tail feather, not enough,
and when I finally catch him,
he has blood on his head
and trembles in my hands,
and this time I take him out
to where Sky waits, impatient with me,
and I say, "I'm sorry, I'm sorry,"
and Sun puts tears in my eyes
while Magpie makes a trail
through the air that I
can never follow.

I try to think of everything,
but Sun pokes me in the eye,
and Sky leans on me,
and my thoughts are very small.

Magpie thinks only of flying
if he thinks at all.

ξ

David Baker

Works and Days

             More in number, five
or six at a time
perched atop stiff cat-

             tail tufts or calling
from lush caverns in
the willow limbs—more

             on the wing, more flash
and blood, more wild song,
who seldom travel

             in numbers bigger
than a pair—the red-
wings returning this

             spring to the park pond
have surprised us all.
It's supposed to be

             a bad time for birds.
El Niño has smeared
California

             for months, spreading east
and windward its strain
of killer drought, of

             greenhouse-effect storms.
A few blocks away
the factory mill

             dusts our own fields with
a mineral mist—
pesticide spills from

            the well-water taps.
The honeybees are
dying out and what-

            ever food these birds
are used to has thinned
next to nothing: yet

            here they are, bright as
bobbers, floating the
rich, brown surfaces.

            It's a windless day
of someone's childhood.
Small wonder so many

            of us have come
to sun with the red-
wings on the flat bank.

            The birds, to see us,
must think all is well,
to see so many

            so happy to be
here—, to see so many
  more gathering now.

ξ

Snowies and Blues

Where there is no accumulation, laced and soft, come flocks
of snowies to shrub pine, wetlands and dock.

Is it a wish to speak a season's complete possibility or make
familiar an inclination to leave? Snowy egrets could be milk or paint
egrets, trillium or salt egrets. But they descend softly,

long necks and wing fans. Each one a blizzard
in a nickname. Is it their lurking extinction, their long,

millennial disintegration that turns blue whales to blues
on biologist tongues? When they call it tracking blues—passing
sonar over the hemispheres one by one and ticking off
fewer mammals than a population can trust, do they know

they're speaking double? Whose blues permeate this air,
whose mammal memory haunts farthest?

ξ

A Prayer for Birds Dying in Darkness and in Light
from The Audubon Society Encyclopedia of North American Birds

These words are sacred to the memory of one
rail bird, flying full throttle, tracing the prairie's throat
up a slight rise, over the cornflowers, into barbed wire.

And also to the memory of one golden eagle, age two,
caught in a leg trap in the Willamette marsh, and seven
semi-palmated plovers killed in seven nights' migration,
striking the shuttered lighthouse in Newport.

For the osprey who dove and locked his talons too deep
in the side of a king salmon, for the salmon who swam down
away from the horrifying sky, for the drowning of the osprey,
the dying of the salmon, hear our prayer.

For the airborne weasel who bit the redtail who carried it
aloft, or the captured rattlesnake who bit the redtail who bit it first;
for the two dead redtails, a moment of silence.

(See Stoddard and Norris [1967] for a list of 29,400 birds
killed in migration at a Florida TV tower. See Crawford [1974]
for reports of an additional 5,550 birds killed at the same tower.)

Deliver the migrating owl from the piercing antenna,
the darting swallow from the lethal golfball, the rose-breasted
grosbeak from the picture windows, no lifeprint sliding down the glass.

Consider the ravens of the air, and how they are fed,
and how they are fed strychnine. The common crossbill loves
the salt spread on highways to melt the ice. The red crossbill,
the evening grosbeak too. Bright corpses cover the median strips.

Bless the robins and waxwings drunk on chinaberries,
fluttering on their backs, the fluid from fermented fruit
running from their mouths.

Tina Kelley

Rest in peace, ring-necked pheasant killed or worse
by the mowing machine. (One male survived with both feet cut
off and was in good health when shot by a hunter.)

Ask intercessions for the northern gannet who choked
on the spiny gurnard, the dorsal fin too cruel for the throat.
The next island over, an old eider starved when the mussel
closed its shell on his tongue.

Heroic, the flock of common loons that landed
on the destroyer's deck, wings encased in ice. Ill-fated,
the yellow-throated warbler flying through the cypress lagoon,
entangled in the golden web of the Carolina silk spider,
looking back and forth to the seven nearest leaves, dying.

An hour of silence for the five million Lapland longspurs,
dead in a snowstorm, March 13 and 14, 1904, landing in quiet
throes over Indiana stubblefields.

Beware, tiny ones, of flying too low into high flipping
waves, of alighting at noon on hot asphalt roofs. The fuzz of
your feathers, the color of bathtub rings, soddens down to
damp dirt. Creatures who weigh nothing die, rot, soak up rain,
become heavy.

Blessed be the ruby-throated hummingbird, impaled
on purple flowers of pasture thistle, or caught by dragonflies,
snatched by frogs, caught by praying mantises.

Remember the robin who returned to the same Maine
yard two summers in a row, a twig sticking out of her back.
Consider one robin in the trap in New York, the large thorn
in its throat.

For American kestrels, the leading causes of death
include mobs of bluejays, cats, lightning, windows, cars, and
locomotives. And lest we forget, the barred owl iced in her
hole, slowly dying as the snow fell beyond her final window,
fast and wide, like champagne bubbles, only downwards.

Prayers rise, like smoke, like birds. Heaven, deliver
them. Life, show them mercy. Circumstance, be kindly.
May they die in their sleep, warm in their nests, or folded
in the sea.

Battering Robin Syndrome

He has split his beak on my view.
He has left his selfprint, almost art.
My window is torturing him.
My hubcaps incense him.

The robin wants my spring yard
to himself. Each reflection's
a rival and must be fought full force.
Each reflection is harder than his skull.

He slides down, hobbles, tries again.
What business do I have holding mirrors
up to nature? It revolts. It suicides.
My love of flat, clear and shining

surfaces, flatter, clearer, shinier than lakes,
than anything in nature, is unnatural,
antinatural. And if nature held mirrors to me,
showed me someone I thought would steal

my truelove, or showed me how I'm doing,
what would I do, would I learn,
or beat my head against her skull,
or try to smash myself against the news?

ξ

Once a Green Sky

A deer was on Linwood and I asked the forest
to come and retrieve her, curl its slow hammers
around our houses and decipher brick into scraps
of clay. My hardest wishes are for and against

ourselves, delicate locusts, ravenous flowers
with an appetite for even the breaths
between the spaces. Say you are alone. Pretend
everyone emulates you. Imagine if alone

the idea of the conversion van, the strong touch
of burrito wafting from the bodega, never
germinated in the cavernous brain. Hands
are no more clever than kneading dough,

the weapon of choice is sleep, the gods we adore
eat their own ribs, supplicant postures
of apology break out simultaneously in each
cabin and in exactly the same way. Impossible, okay,

move on. What if instead I owned one TV
and shared it with you on weekends, Lucille Ball
eating chocolate after chocolate as we laugh
in tribal reflex. If there was just one car

we touched the third Sunday of each month,
licked the leather seats, turned the engine
over and ran behind the bushes, terrified
at the growling dog we'd created, could this be

enough? There's a surprise in all flesh, this
is the purpose of eyes, to find and convey shock.
The deer and I faced as mistakes of context,
errors of intention, and she shot into the same

confusion one street over, we are saints
of replication, my house is your house, my
pierced navel your erection, the deer sniffed
for the green mist, thrashed through an archipelago

of false indicators, islands of shrubs that lasted
five paces, ten breaths, until she ran
into the mouth of a Saturn. From skulls I know
the architecture of her bones, lacy nostrils,

the torsion grooves of ligaments, just as kissing
a shoulder I have faith in the cup
and ball that work the joint, making it curl
into pleasure. I can't shrug gravity, the Holy

Spirit Force, but if possible would dream
silks of what contains us, the habit to make,
to adore the crystal chandelier
whose frail music each day is a dirge

for a hundred species. What if the forest
followed the deer, not into death but through
my living room, what if the rain ate my den
and you and I, unrolling a set of blueprints,

realized the sky is aspiration enough? Or if you
and I, reaching for a vowel, for the last
piece of coal on the stack, gave
silence, gave the eventual diamond back.

ع

Poisoned Dog

The poison had returned him to us
from the upper fields where week-long
in the heavy odor of something wronged

and hunted he'd lost himself.
Now in one spasm on the kitchen floor
his forelegs gave way, the body

trying to shiver the death out of itself,
contracting there, too finely stiff
for any good to come its way or ours.

We saw how his eyes had become wholly his,
and neither the moon shone against them
nor did the wind tend to his fur

like any good master. It was night
and he was dead, stripped even of
the dignity one can come to by dying.

Outside, the animals I imagined
under leaf-cover and limb retreated
toward the one earth that would soak them up,

and believing that nothing but morning
and a hard burial would set things right,
we turned away to climb the stairs:

I remembered then how my uncle,
once lost in the desert, turned also
but to watch two wild dogs one after another,

homing in on the blood they could scent
and spill, come after him like a dream,
and as the first leapt up to his throat

he caught it with a kick, soccer-style,
and sent both yelping back into the madness
of the desert, grateful perhaps

for the knowledge of what one leg
could muscle out and hold at bay,
my uncle grateful too

for what had been spared to go on.
Such magic failed us here: what lay corrupted
was by corruption felled, fallen, and held.

As we slept closer for the feel of it, above him,
we dreamt through our entanglements
of the neighbor's fields poisoned with bad meat,

the scent of dark blooms drifting in
toward our porches, backdoors, even
into our kitchens, until all houses

seemed fit for the dead to enter,
and the house of the dog lay quietest
among all else in its dreaming,

and by daylight, no death
seemed too obvious, and none was forgotten,
or likened to any other.

ξ

For a Newborn Muskrat

It has risen now, just now, to the surface
   Of the muddy water and keeps itself
     Afloat, just barely, by an already floating
Stem of marsh bellflower, the pale claws
   Of one nearly hairless forefoot wavering there,
     Above the flooded den where its mother
Is going to think of something else. It stretches
   Forward with another half-webbed foot
     And draws it back again into a dream
Of swimming, of imagining no longer
   Holding on to the stem, its half-shut eyes
     Dark between pink lids as it takes in
One breath, and another after
   Another, takes in the cloudy light of the ditch
     By the logging road and the old light of the world.

ξ

Invocation

This August night, raccoons,
come to the back door
burnished all summer by salty,
human touch: enter secretly & eat.

Listen, little mask-faced ones,
unstealthy bandits whose tails
are barred with dusk:
listen, gliding green-eyed ones:
I concede you gladly
all this much-handled stuff,
garbage, grain,
the cropped food and cropped heart—
may you gnaw in contentment
through the sleep-hours
on everything left out.

May you find the house
hospitable,
well-used,
stocked with sufficient goods.
I'll settle with your leavings,

as you have settled for mine,
before startling back into darkness
that marks each of us so differently.

ξ

Raccoon Mother

I still remember the night,
your face.
You stay in the lightless
recesses of a weathered heart
that holds the time
we shared as the glowing eyes
of your children watched
—stunned, I cried,
wanting druid powers—
these limited hands,
somehow wet with the blood.
Was this one your favorite?
As if a mother would admit it.
The child would not move
under your flustered prodding.
You looked at me without hatred
—only despair, frail hope.
Too small for this failure,
I had no magic.
Into the space between us
I whispered, This one is gone;
leave with your other children.
The asphalt line that cut
the forest into small places
was no place for a mother.
With young feet following
from the bushes,
you turned and left,
looking back at that spot, and me,
and the quiet beneath my tears?—
one saved for sadder moments
such as these.

ξ

Richard Levine

Encroaching

Without moving, your image
clarified the cemetery dark —
eyes, cowl, stripes — peering
through bars that striated

a sycamore's sheltering
night-shade. Serene
in your fragile wildness,
you crouched on the brink

of MacDonald Avenue's four lanes —
braved for a garbage-night meal.
Do you know this cage you see
me in is made of craving?

ξ

Economics

It began when our last cat died,
struck down as he climbed a post,
dead when he hit the ground. Since then
chipmunks have reclaimed it all: lawn,
woodpile, garden, rock wall; developing
a taste for green beans, spouting peas,
even grass seed. We set live traps, swearing
to transport furry free-loaders to some
Botany Bay across the pond. But we found
we lacked the will to send them to
an unknown fate, to orphan offspring, displace
distant relatives, instigate territorial
disputes. A night in jail might reform them,
so we let them go, reset the traps.

Snap! They're back! And back again, until
it seems we've changed these savages
to civilized sweat-shop squirrels, scurrying
from nine to five. We take the traps away
and leave the bait. They learn quickly —
or do we? The garden's their hostage now
and tributes are demanded every day. Is this
welfare or the tax we pay for society?

ξ

Coyote

Because an occasional cat
doesn't make it out of
the hedges, neighbors are signing
petitions to have you relocated.
Once you were seen as a return
to order, a natural check on the deer,
saving so many Volvos and Saabs.
Now rumor says that you connive
like thieves in backyards and alleys,
pushing the limits of probation.
Your appetite is too close to home
and no one's citing your loyalty
to your mate anymore, who must
fatten by March to raise the young.
But why aren't we asking
what the neighborhood will be like
when you're not out there again
lifting a voice against the silence
of these winter nights?—
Though I'll be left out of summer's
block party for saying this.

ξ

Nine White Ducks

Nine white ducks with blue bills
are laughing together under the mulberry tree.

As I pass with my hoe in my hand,
they stop and look up — a silence of shining black eyes.

There are mulberries enough
to last for a hundred thousand years, and they know it.

Even the little drake that the dog got by the neck —
its voice like a bullfrog's now —

it too has been laughing all morning.
Oh, sweet blue seedy juice! Oh, summer!

But now every feather is frozen in place
as my shadow passes (so dark, the human errand),

and I suddenly see what they see:
from out on the end of the handle I carry

hangs what looks like the foot of a duck.

ξ

Winter Burn

Swathed paths shaping it into triangles,
the field's arching grasses huddle together
with only their seedless caps molested by the wind
that sickles fire across their legs and with a blink-
quick blade blackens their faces.

Then running screaming and feather-burned
wild turkeys burst like angered velociraptors
from the fringes and pound with lunging thighs
their claws across the shorn divide and waterless
creekbed into the grove of leafless willows.

Winter snow will settle the arching coils of soot
into the soil for Spring's green reprieve,
will calm aside the broken columns to, in its melting,
betray a smoke-choked mouse, petrified half-emerged
from its hole, its tiny ears flame-licked.

ξ

City Animals

Just before the tunnel, the train
lurches through a landscape
snatched from a dream. Flame blurts

from high up on the skeletal refinery,
all pipes and tanks. Then a tail of smoke.

The winter twilight looks like fire, too,

smeared above the bleached grasses
of the marsh, and in the shards of water

where an egret the color of newspaper
holds perfectly still, like a small angel

come to study what's wrong with the world.

In the blond reeds, a cat picks her way
from tire to oil drum,

hunting in the petrochemical stink.

Row of nipples, row of sharp ribs.
No fish in the iridescence.
Maybe a sick pigeon, or a mouse.

Across the Hudson,
Manhattan's black geometry begins to spark

as the smut of evening rises in the streets.

Somewhere in it,
a woman with a plastic bag in her hand
follows a dachshund in a purple sweater,

letting him sniff a small square of dirt
studded with cigarette butts.
And in the park a scarred Doberman

drags on his choke chain toward another fight,

but his master yanks him back.
It's like the Buddhist vision of the beasts
in their temporary afterlife, each creature

locked in its own cell of misery,
the horse pulling always uphill
with its terrible load, the whip

flicking bits of skin from its back,
the cornered bear woofing with fear,

the fox's mouth red from the leg in the trap.

Animal islands, without comfort between them.
Which shall inherit the earth?

Not the interlocking kittens frozen in the trash.

Not the dog yapping itself to death
on the twentieth floor. And not the egret,
fishing in the feculent marsh

for the condom and the drowned gun.

No, the earth belongs to the spirits
that haunt the air above the sewer grates,

the dark plumes trailing the highway's
diesel moan, the multitudes
pouring from the smokestacks of the citadel

into the gaseous ocean overhead.

Where will the angel rest itself?
What map will guide it home?

ξ

Jugging

What fur seals and sea otters do
better than any other creatures.

Fold flippers across their chests,
and drift to sleep on the waves,

floating closer and closer in
the early light, the waves rolling

into deep hollows, before one huge
one rises, high above, buries them

for a moment, while I fall off
my flatboard, and hear them

bark as they come up behind my
back, then hurl themselves past,

leaving me with a bump on the back
of my head, the tip of my tongue

bitten, and something brought up
from below that looks at me, too.

It will get worse, it seems to say.
What will? Why? I go on and on with

such questions till a cloud opens
a crack at the far end of the sky.

I have no ideas left, of anything.
Of what's left to see, or imagine.

ξ

Diane Thiel

Echolocations

The waters compassed me about, even to the soul:
the depth closed me round about,
the weeds were wrapped about my head.
(Jonah 2:5)

In Boca Vieja, on the unsettled stretch of beach
which formed the border between two continents,
a coast where water flowed down from the forest—
I had come to find the furthest distance.
At the end of a labyrinth of fallen boulders,
I came upon the massive skeleton,
the whitened frame reflecting back the sun.
The ribcage formed a passage to the sea,
where thin rivers ran between the bones,
dividing further as they reached the ocean.
The skull, half-buried in the sand, resembled
a house from some forgotten fairy tale.
I climbed in through the porthole of an eye,
looked out the double circles filled with light.

I found my way down what was once her throat
and wandered through the gallery of bones.
Her ribcage framed the sea, the sky, the trees—
each canvas a vast range of blues and greens.
I reached the place that must have held her heart,
knowing, as a child, I could have fit inside
her vessels, even. I could have hidden there.
The tide was coming in, reclaiming things
clinging to the curved bones or roaming the shore—
the tiny hydroid forests with their medusae,
the limpets like small traveling volcanoes,
the scrolled whelks, drawing their maze of whorls,
only to be washed away. This was the end
of the whale's road. She passed her life to thousands.

I felt the sun-warm bone against my skin—
and a sudden heartbeat in the skeleton.
Her heart beat with a distant beckoning,
and in a moment I was with her, traveling
the hwaelweg, the road itself another kenning.
The ocean set the cadence, the swells singing
a line, receiving back another line—
in each reply, the slightest variation.
Our languages returning to the sounds
encoded in our strands, the spiral towers
of our helixes spinning round each other.
The calls reverberating through the waters
to navigate the depths, to guide us through
one ocean to another, the dark indigos,

the song returning from the deepest blues.

$$\xi$$

Boca Vieja: (Old Mouth), Pacific Coast, Colombia
hwaelweg: whale-road, Old English kenning

My Brother the Javelina

Nights I jockey a Peterbilt across
the Texas panhandle, my bones an implosion
of weary woe, cantaloupes by the ton
mellowing in refrigeration, any company
is much welcome. Other truckers
over strong black coffee tell me how
DeSoto's conquistadors on mustang
ponies often appear over starlit scrub.
Minds can go awry it seems anywhere
alone along this naked Interstate.
But I count myself among the sane.
And living. Slowing en route to Taos
that eerie hour ghosts stir up a fuss,
I scan the storm-gutted arroyos,
catching amber orbs, meerschaum tusks,
bristled ruffs. Cab window down, elbow
hanging out, I let out championship
hogcalls. Once husky squeals skirr back,
I relax — it's my brother the javelina.

Approaching Judea

I am told there are no moose in Judea; but I
have seen them, thousands and thousands of them.
— Shaya Kline

I've been in this desert
longer than I care to
admit to any of you. I haven't
eaten a bite since I left Jerusalem,
unless you count the sand
the wind keeps throwing in my face.
I came here for the moose,
though everyone I've asked continues
to insist moose have never been here
and never will be. I don't care
for that kind of talk. I'm convinced
moose can get along anywhere. And where
better than here, a holy land
for the holiest of beasts? I admit,
I nearly gave up, girded my sandy loins
for the long walk out. But last night,
I was awakened from my pillow of sand
to a strange calling, a low sound
like wind, but with blood in it.
And as I stared blindly into the black world,
the moon lifted from behind a dune, lighting up
an entire desert of moose, their shaggy heads
all lifted and calling out their one, holy word.

ξ

India Cows

In Ahmadebad, an old city
where Ghandi had his ashram,
the cows lie all day on the median
between the lanes of frantic traffic.
The exhaust keeps the insects away.
At dusk the cows rise all together
and mosey to the garbage dumps
where the faithful have put out
food and water. They call it
"feeding the god." It's good,
I think, to have a god to feed,
who knows hunger and the
ways of the world.

For the Animal Rights Activists

I want to whisper something reed-like for those activists
who keep so much trust in love,

so much trust in an unknown spirit set beneath a skin,
and in the song, denied, which hides behind a ribcage,

which is missed in the unfamiliar eye. How beautiful,
those activists, who leap from safety nets and into fires,

raise a snuffed voice and pray to the smoke for reshaping,
who mouth the tiny spirals of our ears, biting them uncurled.

For them I want to whisper something flute shaped
that may be no surprise, like:

Our souls have abandoned our bodies;

our souls are starved brown children
digging bowl shapes in the dirt beneath old fences;

our souls have slipped away with slivers in their lips,
with sonatas of stolen ivory, with arias from nests, with cavatinas;

and then, our souls are stretched leather, then, wrinkled
black boots, running from the trenches round our feet.

If only we would learn to let them wear us, not the reverse.
If only we could love the empty, angry stomachs in our souls

like those activists, whose tongues are never sated,
whose sheets are often knotted by a lack of sleep,

whose mattresses are holding tanks where dreams begin to filter
through the flesh and sink into the fields of their sternums.

If only we would want to know with firmness
what they know, but oh we cannot seem to see at night,

if only we could swallow, move the darkness through our throats,
and fill ourselves with a softness such as theirs.

ξ

Notes on the Contributors

Austin Alexis has published work in *Barrow Street, The Writer, The Journal, Connecticut River Review* and other magazines. He has work forthcoming in the Dana Literary Society On-line Journal. He has been a fellow at the Millay Colony for the Arts and the Helene Wurlitzer Foundation of New Mexico.

David Baker is the author of eight books, most recently *Changeable Thunder* (2001, poems) and *Heresy and the Ideal: On Contemporary Poetry* (2000, criticism), both from the University of Arkansas Press. He teaches at Denison University and is Poetry Editor of *The Kenyon Review*.

Will M. Baker is a graduate student at Mills College in Oakland, California. This is his first publication.

Ellen Bass's new book is *Mules of Love* (BOA Editions, 2002). She has published four previous volumes of poetry -- *I'm Not Your Laughing Daughter, Of Separateness and Merging, For Earthly Survival*, and *Our Stunning Harvest*. Among her awards for poetry are the Elliston Book Award from the University of Cincinnati, The Pablo Neruda Prize from *Nimrod*/Hardman, and the Larry Levis Prize from *Missouri Review*. Her poems have appeared in *The Beloit Poetry Journal, DoubleTake, Field*, and others.

Randy Blasing's *Second Home*, his sixth book of verse, is from Copper Beech. Persea Books will soon issue a revised and enlarged edition of his *Poems of Nazim Hikmet*.

William Borden is a poet, novelist, playwright, and essayist. His poem, *Eurydice's Song*, was published in 1999 by St. Andrew's Press, and a chapbook, *Slow Step and Dance*, was published by Loonfeather Press. His novel, *Superstoe*, was recently republished by Orloff Press. The film version of his play, *The Last Prostitute*, was shown on Lifetime Television and is on video.

Grace Butcher is the editor of *The Listening Eye* and Professor Emeritus of English at Kent State University Geauga Campus. Her work has appeared in *Best American Poetry 2000* and many magazines and anthologies since the mid-60's.

Scott Cairns teaches poetry writing, American literature, and seminars in poetry and poetics at the University of Missouri-Columbia. His five poetry collections are *Philokalia: New & Selected Poems* (2002), *Recovered Body* (1998), *Figures for the Ghost* (1994), *The Translation of Babel* (1990), and *The Theology of Doubt* (1985). His poems have appeared in *Best Spiritual Writing* in 1998 and 2000, in *Upholding Mystery* (Oxford '97), in *Best of Prairie Schooner* (UNP, 2001), and in a host of literary magazines such as *The Paris Review, The Atlantic Monthly, The New Republic,* and *Image: A Journal of the Arts and Religion.*

Ashley Capps received her M. A. in English from Ohio University in 2002 and is currently the Jay C. and Ruth Halls Poetry Fellow at the Wisconsin Writer's Institute. This is her first publication.

Robert M. Chute's seventh chapbook, *Sweeping The Sky*, a letter press production by Wolfe Editions, deals with Soviet women combat pilots in WWII. His current project is a three language reissue of *Thirteen Moons: in English, French, and Passamaquoddy.*

Tom Crawford's books are *I Want To Say Listen* (Ironwood Press), *If It Weren't for Trees* (Lynx House Press), *Lauds* (Cedar House Books), *China Dancing* (Cedar House Books), and *The Temple On Monday* (Eastern Washington University Press). He has received Two NEAs for poetry and the Oregon Literary Book Award for *Lauds* in 1996.

Deborah Cummins is the author of *Beyond the Reach* (BkMk Press, forthcoming in 2002) and *From the Road it Looks Like Paradise* (State Street Books, 1997). She is the recipient of numerous fellowships and awards including a James Michener fellowship, the Washington Prize in fiction, the Headwaters Prize in poetry, and a Literary Award from the Illinois Arts Council. She is the President of the Modern Poetry Association in Chicago.

J. P. Dancing Bear's poems have appeared in hundreds of magazines and journals including the *Clackamas Literary Review, Borderlands: The Texas Poetry Review, The Mid-America Poetry Review,* and *The Midwest Poetry Review.* His chapbook, *What Language*, won the 2002 chapbook prize from *Slipstream* magazine and press. He hosts a weekly poetry program on public radio 91.5 FM, KKUP, Cupertino, and is Editor-in-Chief of *The DMQ Review.*

Gregory Djanikian directs the undergraduate creative writing program at the University of Pennsylvania. His four collections of poems are *The Man in the Middle, Falling Deeply into America, About Distance*, and most recently, *Years Later* (2000), all published by Carnegie-Mellon.

Joseph Duemer has published three books of poetry, *Customs* (University of Georgia Press, 1986), *Static* (Owl Creek Press, 1996) and *Magical Thinking* (Ohio State University Press, winner of the 2001 OSU / The Journal Award in Poetry). His poems have appeared in *American Poetry Review, The Antioch Review, Boulevard, Field, The Georgia Review, The Iowa Review, Manoa* and other journals. He teaches Humanities, Literature & Creative Writing at Clarkson University.

Stephen Dunn is the author of eleven collections of poems, including *Different Hours* (Norton), winner of the 2001 Pulitzer Prize. Other awards include NEA and Guggenheim fellowships, several Woodrow Wilson Fellowships in Poetry, the Lila Wallace Fellow in Poetry, the Academy Award in Literature, the Levinson Award from Poetry, the James Wright Prize, The Iowa Review Subscribers Award, National Endowment for the Arts Creative Writing Fellowship, and Distinguished Artist Fellowship and Creative Writing Fellowships from the New Jersey State Council on the Arts. His poems have been published in such periodicals as *The Atlantic Monthly, The Nation, the New Republic, the New Yorker*, and *the American Poetry Review*, among many others.

Karl Elder is the author of five collections of poetry, including the newly released *The Geocryptogrammatist's Pocket Compendium of the United States*. He has recently been nominated for a Pushcart Prize for the third time in his career, having won the award in 2001. His work appears in *The Best American Poetry 2000* and *September 11, 2001: American Writers Respond* from Etruscan Press. He is Fessler Professor of Creative Writing at Lakeland College.

Sally Fisher's poetry has appeared in *Chelsea, Field, New Directions, Poetry East, Shenandoah, Tar River*, and other magazines and anthologies. Composer Paul Alan Levi has set a group of her poems to music. The New Amsterdam Singers gave the premiere performance at Merkin Concert Hall in May 2002.

Lisa Fishman's poems have appeared in *The Antioch Review, The Beloit Poetry Journal, Colorado Review, Crazyhorse, The Indiana Review, Louisiana Literature, Poetry Northwest, The Prairie Schooner, The Wallace Stevens Journal*, and elsewhere. Her book is *The Deep Heart's Core is a Suitcase* (New Issues Press, 1996).

Stuart Friebert's book of poems, *Funeral Pie*, won the Four Way Book Award in 1997. His work has appeared recently in *The Massachusetts Review* and *Gulf Coast*.

Dan Gerber's work has been published in a wide variety of magazines and journals, including *The New Yorker, The Nation, The Georgia Review, Tricycle* and *Poetry*. He was the recipient of the Michigan Author Award in 1992, had work selected for *The Best American Poetry 1999*, and received The Mark Twain Award for distinguished contributions to Midwestern Literature in 2001. His most recent collection of poems is *Trying to Catch the Horses* (Michigan State University Press, 1999).

Jason Gray received his MA from the Writing Seminars of Johns Hopkins University. His poetry and nonfiction have appeared in *Poetry, The Threepenny Review, Literary Imagination, Prairie Schooner*, and *Antenna Magazine*.

Bob Hicok's latest book of poems, *Animal Soul* (Invisible Cities, 2001) was a finalist for the National Book Critics Circle Award. His work has appeared in *The New Yorker, Boulevard, The American Poetry Review, The Iowa Review, The Southern Review, The Pushcart Prize XXV*, two editions of *The Best American Poetry*, and other publications.

Jane Hirshfield is the author of five collections of poetry: *Alaya, Of Gravity and Angels, The October Palace, The Lives of the Heart,* and *Given Sugar, Given Salt*. Her awards include the Poetry Center Book Award, the Bay Area Book Award, the Commonwealth Club of California's Poetry Medal, and fellowships from the Guggenheim and Rockefeller foundations. Her work has appeared in *The Best American Poetry, The Pushcart Prize Anthology, The Atlantic Monthly, The Nation, The New Yorker, The New Republic* and many literary periodicals.

Amy Holman lives in New York and directs the Literary Horizons program at Poets & Writers, Inc. Her poetry has been published in numerous magazines in print and online, including *Literal Latte, Poet Lore, 4th Street, Aileron, Mystic River Review, CrossConnect* and *Failbetter*. She's also had poetry and prose published in the *1999 Best American Poetry, The Second Word Thursdays Anthology*, and the uniquely packaged Espresso Press anthology, *The History of Panty Hose In America*.

Tina Kelley is a late-night reporter for the Metro section of the New York Times. Her first book, *The Gospel of Galore*, is due out in the fall of 2002 from Word Press. Her poems have appeared in numerous magazines and journals including *The Beloit Poetry Journal, Poetry Northwest*, and *Prairie Schooner*.

John Kennedy teaches freshman composition and English at Quinnipiac University in Connecticut. His book reviews appear regularly in *The Antioch Review*; his poems and reviews have appeared in *Poetry, Prairie Schooner, North American Review, The Seattle Review, The Texas Review, The Chicago Review*, et cetera. His poetry chapbook, *How To Be a Witness*, is from Picadilly Press, Fayetteville, Arkansas.

Ted Kooser is the author of nine collections of poetry, most recently *Winter Morning Walks: 100 Postcards to Jim Harrison* (Carnegie Mellon University Press, 2000). His work has appeared in *The New Yorker, Poetry, The American Poetry Review, The Hudson Review, Kansas Quarterly, The Kenyon Review, Antioch Review, Midwest Quarterly, Prairie Schooner, Poetry Northwest, Prairie Schooner, Shenandoah, Tailwind, Cream City Review* and elsewhere. He has received two NEA fellowships in poetry, the Pushcart Prize, the Stanley Kunitz Prize, The James Boatwright Prize, and a Merit Award from the Nebraska Arts Council.

Steve Kowit's books include *The Dumbell Nebula* (Heyday Books, 2000), *In the Palm of Your Hand: The Poet's Portable Workshop* (Tilbury House, 1995), and *The Maverick Poets* (Gorilla Press, 1984). His work has appeared in *The Los Angeles Times* and *The New Yorker* as well as many other magazines and anthologies including *The Literary Review, Ploughshares*, and Czeslaw Milosz's *The Book of Luminous Things*. His awards include the NEA, The Pushcart, and San Diego Lifetime Literary Achievement Award.

Richard Levine is the author of *What Light Will Bring, Poems*, published by Rattapallax Press.

Sarah Lindsay works as a copy editor in Greensboro, North Carolina. Her book *Primate Behavior* was a finalist for the National Book Award in 1997. Her second collection is *Mount Clutter* (Grove Press, 2002). Her poems have appeared in many fine magazines including *The Paris Review*.

Edward C. Lynskey is the author of one volume of poems titled *The Tree Surgeon's Gift* (Scripta, 1990). His short fiction and poems have appeared or are forthcoming in such publications as *Poetry Northwest, The Atlantic Monthly, Fables, Zuzu's Petals Quarterly, Artemis Magazine, 3 AM, Vacancy, Demensions Zine, Planet Magazine, Quantum Muse*, and *New Letters*.

Wesley McNair is the recipient of fellowships from the Rockefeller, Fulbright, and Guggenheim Foundations, an NEH fellowship in literature, and two NEA Fellowships for Creative Writers. Other honors include the Devins Award; prizes in poetry from *Poetry, Poetry Northwest*, and *Yankee* magazines; and the Sarah Josepha Hale Medal, for his "distinguished contribution to the world of letters". His work has appeared in the *Pushcart Prize* annual, two editions of *The Best American Poetry*, and over forty anthologies and textbooks. His most recent volumes of verse are the dual reprint *The Town of No & My Brother Running* (Godine, 1997), *Talking in the Dark* (Godine, 1998), a reissue of his first collection, *The Faces of Americans in 1853*, by Carnegie Mellon University Press in its Classic Contemporaries series (2001), and *Fire* (Godine, 2002). In addition, he has edited a volume of contemporary writing in Maine titled *Quotable Moose*.

Jane Mead is the author of two collections of poetry, most recently *House of Poured-Out Waters* from University of Illinois Press (2001). She is the recipient of grants from the Lannan and Whiting Foundations, and poet-in-residence at Wake Forest University in Winston-Salem, North Carolina.

Alyce Miller's work has most recently appeared in *Iowa Review, The Sun, Witness, Massachusetts Review, Story Quarterly, New Letters,* and *Puerto del Sol*. She is the author of two books of fiction, a novel, *Stopping for Green Lights* (Doubleday 1999), and a collection of short stories, *The Nature of Longing* (Norton 1995), winner of the Flannery O'Connor Award for Fiction. Her work has also been awarded the *Kenyon Review* Award for Literary Excellence and the Lawrence Foundation Prize (*Michigan Quarterly Review*). Ms. Miller is a professor of English and creative writing at Indiana University in Bloomington, faculty advisor to Speak Out for Animals, and president of the Animal Legal Defense Fund chapter at Indiana University Law School.

Robert S. Pesich is an associate editor for *The Montserrat Review*. Recent work has appeared in *The Bitter Oleander, Mediphors*, and *Albatross*. His chapbook, *Burned Kilim*, was published in August 2001 by Dragonfly Press.

Kenneth Pobo's book, *Ordering: A Season in My Garden*, is from Higganum Hills Books. His work has appeared in *Nimrod, Colorado Review, Mudfish, Blue Unicorn, Indiana Review*, and elsewhere.

Lawrence Raab is the author of five collections of poetry, including *What We Don't Know about Each Other* (Penguin, 1993), a winner of the National Poetry Series and finalist for the National Book Award. His poems have appeared in such periodicals as *The New Yorker, The Atlantic Monthly, The Kenyon Review, The Nation*, and *The Paris Review*.

Carl Rakosi's *The Collected Poems of Carl Rakosi* was published in 1986 by the National Poetry Foundation. His *Poems 1923-1941* (Sun and Moon Press) won the PEN Center USA West award in 1996.

David Roderick is a Wallace Stegner Fellow in Poetry at Stanford University. His poetry, fiction, and essays have appeared in several journals and magazines.

C. J. Sage's poetry collection is *Let's Not Sleep* (Dream Horse Press, 2002). Her poems have appeared in *The Threepenny Review, Smartish Pace, The Spoon River Poetry Review, The Seattle Review, Light Quarterly* and many other magazines. Her awards include the Academy of American Poets Prize, several Phelans, and the Marjorie McLaughlin Folendorf Award for outstanding achievement in creative writing.

Gary Short has been a Stegner Fellow at Stanford and a resident of the Fine Arts Work Center in Provincetown. He is the author of *Theory of Twilight* and a second book of poems, *Flying Over Sonny Liston*, which won the Western States Book Award. He is from Nevada and has been on the staff of the Foothill Writers Conference and the Art of the Wild Conference.

Thomas R. Smith's latest book of poems is *The Dark Indigo Current* (Holy Cow! Press, 2000). He lives in River Falls, Wisconsin.

Gabriel Spera's work has appeared in *Best American Poetry 2000*, *Poetry, Prairie Schooner,* and others. His book, *The Standing Wave*, was just selected for The National Poetry Series.

Hannah Stein's two books of poetry are *Earthlight* (La Questa Press) and a chapbook, *Schools of Flying Fish*. Her poems have appeared widely in literary journals including *The Antioch Review, the Beloit Poetry Journal, Calyx, Poetry Flash*, and *The Yale Review*. Her poems have won national awards and have been twice nominated for the Pushcart Prize.

Ira Sukrungruang earned a BA at Southern Illinois University and an MFA in creative nonfiction at the Ohio State University. His essays and poems have appeared in *Crab Orchard Review, ACM (Another Chicago Magazine), Fourth Genre, Witness*, and other literary magazines. Currently, he is working on his memoir, *A Normal Thai Son*.

Arthur Sze is the author if six books of poetry and the recipient of numerous awards including a John Simon Guggenheim Memorial Foundation Fellowship, a Lila Wallace-Reader's Digest Writer's Award, a Lannan Literary Award for Poetry, and the National Endowment for the Arts. He lives in New Mexico where he is a Professor of Creative Writing at the Institute of American Indian Arts.

Diane Thiel's book, *Echolocations*, received the 13th Annual Nicholas Roerich Poetry Prize and is published by Story Line Press (2000). Her work has recently appeared in *Poetry, The Hudson Review*, and *Best American Poetry 1999*. Her writing guide, *Writing Your Rhythm: Using Nature, Culture, Form and Myth*, is from Story Line Press. She received a Fulbright for 2001-2002 and teaches at the University of New Mexico.

Chase Twichell's books of poetry include *The Snow Watcher* (Ontario Review Press, 1998), *The Ghost of Eden* (1995), *Perdido* (1991), *The Odds* (1986), and *Northern Spy* (1981). She has won awards from the Artists Foundation (Boston), the New Jersey State Council on the Arts, and the American Academy of Arts and Letters, and fellowships from the Guggenheim Foundation and the National Endowment for the Arts. She taught in the creative writing program at Princeton University from 1989 to 1998 and in the M.F.A. program at Goddard College; she now teaches in the M.F.A. Program for Writers at Warren Wilson College.

David Wagoner has published sixteen books of poetry, most recently *Traveling Light: Collected and New Poems* (University of Illinois Press, 1999), winner of the William Stafford Memorial Award. He has received an American Academy of Arts and Letters award, the Sherwood Anderson Award, the Fels Prize, the Ruth Lilly Poetry Prize, the Eunice Tjetjens Memorial and English-Speaking Union prizes from Poetry, and fellowships from the Ford Foundation, the Guggenheim Foundation, and the National Endowment for the Arts.

Charles Harper Webb's latest book of poems, *Tulip Farms and Leper Colonies*, was published by BOA Editions, Ltd. in 2001. Awards include the Morse Prize, the Kate Tufts Discovery Award, the Whiting Writer's Award, and the Felix Pollak Prize. A 2001-02 Guggenheim Fellow, he teaches at California State University, Long Beach.

Alice Ahrens Williams is co-founder and art director of the *Common Ground Review*. First prize winner in Asnuntuck College's year 2000 poetry competition, she had represented this college on the Student Poetry Circuit of 1997. Her poems have appeared in *Northeast Magazine, The Pine Island Journal, The Common Ground Review, Freshwater*, and A*rt of the Maine Islands: Down East Books* among others. As a finalist in the Sunken Garden Poetry Contest, she was published in *The Hartford Courant's Northeast Magazine* in August of 2001.

ع

Alphabetical Index of Authors

ξ

[1]From *The Seattle Review*, Volume XXIII, Number 3, 2001. Seattle, Washington.

[2]From *Writers Online*, Volume I, Number 3, Spring 1997. http://www.albany.edu/writers-inst/olv1n3.html.

"To Hear the Falling World" is from *Of Gravity and Angels* (Wesleyan University Press, 1988). Reprinted by permission of the author and Wesleyan University Press.

"The Animals of America" first appeared in *Witness*. Reprinted by permission of the author.

"The Puppy" is from *Walking in the Dark* (David R. Godine, 1998). Reprinted by permission of the author.

"Talking to the Dog" first appeared in *Witness*. Reprinted by permission of the author.

"Abandoned Bluetick Bitch" is from *Magical Thinking* (Ohio State University Press, 2001). Reprinted by permission of the author and Ohio State University Press.

"Aisle of Dogs" is from *The Ghost of Eden* (Ontario Review Press, 1995). Reprinted by permission of the author.

"Mourning for Rue" first appeared in *Poetry East*. Reprinted by permission of the author.

"Tormenting the Cat" first appeared in *Witness*. Reprinted by permission of the author.

"Psalm" is from *Flying Over Sonny Liston* (University of Nevada Press). Reprinted by permission of the author.

"Advertisement for the Ford Explorer" first appeared in *River Styx*. Reprinted by permission of the author.

"The Bear on Main Street" is from *Trying to Catch the Horses* (Michigan State University Press, 1999). Reprinted by permission of the author.

"The Deer" is from *After the Reunion* (University of Arkansas Press, 1994). Reprinted by permission of the author.

"Gently Close" first appeared in *The DMQ Review*. Reprinted by permission of the author.

"Cows" first appeared in *The Beloit Poetry Journal*. Reprinted by permission of the author.

"Christmas Lambs" first appeared in *High Plains Literary Review*. Reprinted by permission of the author.

"No One Talks About This" is from *The Collected Poems of Carl Rakosi* (The National Poetry Foundation, 1986). Reprinted by permission of the author and The National Poetry Foundation.

"Passing a Truck Full of Chickens at Night on Highway Eighty" is reprinted from *The Lord and the General Din of the World* by Jane Mead, published by Sarabande Books, Inc. © 1996 by Jane Mead. Reprinted by permission of Sarabande Books and the author.

"In Your Honor" is from *The Redshifting Web: Poems 1970-1998*. Reprinted with the permission of Copper Canyon Press, P. O. Box 271, Port Townsend, WA 98368-0271.

"Sushi" first appeared in *Poetry*. Copyright © 2001 by The Modern Poetry Association. Reprinted by permission of the Editor of *Poetry*.

"The New Fish Store" first appeared in *Poetry East*. Reprinted by permission of the author.

"Harbor Seals" is from *The Theology of Doubt* (Cleveland State University Press, 1985). Reprinted by permission of the author.

"The Bisbee Donkeys" first appeared in *Gulf Coast* and is from the forthcoming *Beyond the Reach* (BkMk Press, 2002). Reprinted by permission of the author.

"Bears in China" first appeared in *The Spoon River Poetry Review*. Reprinted by permission of the author.

"Elephant Waltz" and "The Acts of the Elephants" are from *Primate Behavior* (Grove/Atlantic, Inc., 1997). Reprinted by permission of the author and Grove/Atlantic, Inc.

"Byzantine Bird" first appeared in *Poetry*. Copyright © 2001 by The Modern Poetry Association. Reprinted by permission of the Editor of *Poetry*.

"Narcosis Song" is from *Let's Not Sleep* (Dream Horse Press, 2002). Reprinted by permission of Dream Horse Press.

"Slow Butterflies in the Luminous Field" is from *Mount Clutter* (Grove/Atlantic, Inc., 2002). Reprinted by permission of the author and Grove/Atlantic, Inc.

"Cheese Penguin" is from *Primate Behavior* (Grove/Atlantic, Inc., 1997). Reprinted by permission of the author and Grove/Atlantic, Inc.

"Who'll Say Dugong When the Dugong's Gone?" first appeared in *Witness*. Reprinted by permission of the author.

"His Hot Breath on Her Cheek" is from *Primate Behavior* (Grove/Atlantic, Inc., 1997). Reprinted by permission of the author and Grove/Atlantic, Inc.

"Panda Passing" first appeared in *forpoetry.com*. Reprinted by permission of the author.

"Adam and Eve Go To the Zoo" first appeared in *The Threepenny Review*. Reprinted by permission of the author.

"The Snow Leopard" first appeared in *Poetry*. Copyright © 2000 by The Modern Poetry Association. Reprinted by permission of the Editor of *Poetry*.

"When Peacocks Scream" first appeared in *Witness*. Reprinted by permission of the author.

"How I Learned That My Feet Must Always Be On The Ground" first appeared in *The Seattle Review*. Reprinted by permission of the author.

"Works and Days" is from *Changeable Thunder* (University of Arkansas Press, 2001). Reprinted by permission of the author.

"Snowies and Blues" first appeared in *The Mystic River Review*. Reprinted by permission of the author.

"A Prayer for Birds Dying in Darkness and Light" first appeared in *Poetry Northwest*. Reprinted by permission of the author.

"Battering Robin Syndrome" first appeared in *The Beloit Poetry Journal*. Reprinted by permission of the author.

"Once a Green Sky" is from *Animal Soul* (Invisible Cities Press, 2001). Reprinted by permission of the author.

"Poisoned Dog" is from *The Man in the Middle* (Carnegie-Mellon Press, 1984). Reprinted by permission of the author.

"For a Newborn Muskrat" first appeared in *Witness*. Reprinted by permission of the author.

"Invocation" is from *Of Gravity and Angels* (Wesleyan University Press, 1988). Reprinted by permission of the author and Wesleyan University Press.

"Coyote" is from *How To Be A Witness* (Picadilly Press). Reprinted by permission of the author.

"Nine White Ducks" first appeared in *Witness*. Reprinted by permission of the author.

"City Animals" is from *The Ghost of Eden* (Ontario Review Press, 1996). Reprinted by permission of the author.

"Jugging" first appeared in *Witness*. Reprinted by permission of the author.

"Echolocations" won the 1999 Robert Frost Award and first appeared in *The Dark Horse*. Reprinted by permission of the author.

"My Brother the Javelina" first appeared in *Least Loved Beasts for the Really Wild West: A Tribute* (Native West Press, 1997). Reprinted by permission of the author.

"Approaching Judea" is from *The Theology of Doubt* (Cleveland State University Press, 1985). Reprinted by permission of the author.

"For the Animal Rights Activists" is from *Let's Not Sleep* (Dream Horse Press, 2002). Reprinted by permission of Dream Horse Press.

With special thanks to J. P. Dancing Bear, Bob Hicok, and Steve Kowit.

ξ